Hope Is a Silhouette

A collection of poetry
and art by
Lana McDonagh

Wordville

ISBN: 978-1-7391030-1-9

First edition

Cover and interior artwork by Lana McDonagh. Prints available to buy from Etsy.com/shop/OnlookersArt

Proofread by Ruby Gawe

Wordville
www.wordville.net
info@wordville.net

For my son, Wilde.

'I was going to pick flowers;
Now I leave them all standing'
–Hermann Hesse

About LANA MCDONAGH

Lana McDonagh is an artist and award-winning composer for film and TV. Originally from London, and now based in Sussex, her music has been featured on TV shows, commercials and films across the globe, with credits including 'Black Mirror' and 'You'. **Hope Is a Silhouette** is Lana's debut collection of poetry.

Contents

List of Illustrations

Night-Time Confessional

Some things I only say in the dark
To the ear of the sickle moon

Voicing thoughts out loud
Just to have them marooned

In the thick, treacle silence
of the unconscious you

Secrets set adrift
Unmoored from the mouth

As you breathe in
As you breathe out

My night-time confessional
Uttered under the somnolent glow
Of a heavy velvet sky

The Lock-In

There was Paris
But
All I cared about was that his tongue
  was in my mouth
And that he loved me
My breasts reminded him of the Venus de Milo
He held them
Tenderly at first
And then hungrily
'Will you remember?'

The air in the room grew stale
  as we let four walls hold us captive
Willing prisoners
We bloomed inside that box
As fertile as soil
Seeding stories of all the great things
  we might do with our lives
If we could just make it out
  from underneath the sheets
Sheets that were not our own
but had become
Entangled, linen witnesses

We ate in the dark
Fleshy fruits
Rapacious hands peeling layers back
To reveal soft inside segments

There was Paris
But all I cared about
Was you

Blue under blue skies

Blue Under Blue Skies

Rough callouses and
open blisters
From digging so deep
Rooting yourself a weeping willow
Your head
has almost become indistinguishable
  from the pillow
A brick within epidermis
A hessian sack of pebbles
with a smile sewn askew
Broken button eyes
A face in the mirror that's not quite you
They painted the sky onto the ceiling
As if the weather would help your mood
But you're blue under blue skies
Locked in a room without a view
Why don't you
'Read an inspirational quote or two'
'Wake up tomorrow, start anew?'
Silk gloves slip
On the grip they tell you to get ahold of
Perspective shatters like porcelain
'Open the blinds and let the light come through'
Why don't you
'Shrug the weight off your shoulders?'
Give Atlas back the boulder
'Those sad eyes are making you look older'
As if the indelible stamp of crow's feet
could cajole her
To tighten up the screw

Forget-You Kisses

Not your lips
Feather light and dewy
Eyelashes tickling
The side of my cheek
The curve of my neck and
Sharp ledge of my collarbone;
A diving board from which
You used to leap, so carelessly

Little forget-you kisses
A cleansing detergent
Wiping away
Invisible fingerprints
and
colourless bruises

Our History
Slowly and gently
Becomes insubstantial
After a stranger's sorbet
of
Forget-you kisses

Goosebump Braille

When drain un-blocker becomes
Acid rain
dismantling
Golden brown architecture
Strands of bottle highlights bonded solid
A woven army
Strong enough to choke the pipes
Then, do you miss living alone?

When our bedroom becomes
Glacial and inhospitable
Because I've swaddled myself a baby
And left you without shelter
Covered in nothing but
Goosebump braille
Then, do you miss living alone?

When I become contrary
And argue with a lawyer's conviction
Or lie with the ease of a politician
A missile
In the monotony of modern life
Then, do you miss living alone?

If not then,
When?

Narcissus

Cleopatra wakes me from my slumber and bathes me in milky refractions
She welcomes in the white night
And the satellite
Shadows are cast on my bare chest
Butterflies, rabbits and a sly fox

Limbs unfurl and eyelids unstick
But it is too early
Foetal in fact

Begging for an eclipse
Why has night not quite devoured day?
Like a spoiled child whose belly is too full to finish the food on their plate

Instead of the moon or sun
Or North star
A gilded mirror
My reflection

And it blinds me

Before Me

A dusty layer of snow has settled upon your skin
And I give myself sea legs because there are
  footprints in this snow
and the flakes have compressed
so the crunch of my steps are not as loud
as the ones before me

A pure white expanse
Muddied by another's boot

Involuntary greediness gurgles
Unfulfilled desire swells into a tsunami
  of revulsion
and a primal need for virginal landscapes

I want to traverse your cities
And climb your mountains
Leaving my flag triumphantly at the highest peak

I want an avalanche to lay a fresh sheet of future
So I can hear my weight
As I tread upon the past

Vermillion Red

I was painting in his living room
when it happened

Vermilion red
spilled violently upon his beige carpet
Of all the colours I thought:
Love and
FURY

We fell silent as we looked upon the stain
I thought of Pollock
While he
Bit down on his lip to stop himself from shouting
Vermillion red blood slowly filling his mouth
Bright and metallic

I said 'sorry'
Very quietly
An inaudible whisper
Because I knew I would do it again
Perhaps with cerulean blue
Someday

Retraction

'I love you'

She had only said it
To hear what the sequence of words sounded like
out loud
Holding herself at verbal gunpoint
Forcing her lips to form foreign shapes
Her tongue sliding softly around unfamiliar syllables
It felt like a slow murder
And she wished she had swallowed the sentence instead of
spitting it out
The aftertaste being
Unpalatable
sticky
and
lingering

Wiping her hand slowly across her mouth
She observed the smeared red residue
of a white lie

Forever Visitor

How can we imagine
When they ask how our lives may change
Once the countdown has expired
And I detonate a forever visitor
Into the middle of us

Nearing full bloom
Expanding Ocean Sunfish
We wait for the swollen shuttlecock stomach to still
And listen for the soft whistle of a shrinking balloon
While watching the clock
In sweet anticipation of meeting
the jumping jack
That is
half of me
and half of you

Sunflowers

The sunflowers were a brilliant yellow
But they went brown very quickly
I cried
and he told me that
Picked flowers were just 'perfumed corpses'

I was not sure if we had committed a murder

He told me not to think too much on it
And that heaven sounded like a drag anyway

Tyranny of Routine

Sunday pines
For an endless night
A sanctuary
for closing eyes
The sun betrays us when it rises
Can't outrun
yellow strip lighting

Tomorrow's going to come...
Just like it's always done...
Tomorrow's going to come...

A new day for the masses
But if you can feel time passing
It's a slow-burn down to ashes
Every moment
Everlasting

For some
Tomorrow's going to come...
Tomorrow's going to come...

The routine step onto the carriage
They ask me how I am?
'I'm average'
They say 'you're young and you are able, you have food upon your table'

Am I still young?
Tomorrow's going to come...
Tomorrow's going to come...

Thoughts on Love

You showed me heaven
But I didn’t die

Hope Is a Silhouette

Hope is a silhouette:
A kiss
An unclenched fist
Unexplored horizons
Newborn babies crying
The outline of somebody lying
Next to you

Hope is a silhouette:
A telephone ringing
Bricks and mortar shaped for living
A gambler in the throes of winning
The dawn chorus singing
Floral buds springing up
in between slabs
of solid, grey concrete

Hope is a silhouette:
Hands clasped to pray
Clear X-rays
A caught bouquet
Santa's sleigh
Every cliché
Every cliché

Hope is a silhouette
walking away...

Inner Voices

Soaked in lemony bitterness
Bathed in water that has met the lightning strike
Hot and unbridled
Near foaming at the mouth
The pointed, grinding teeth of a rabid dog
Clenched in jaw-snapping rhythms
A fully weaponised diatribe
Lathered in loathing
Coated in contempt
Draped in dissatisfaction
A self-obsessed suicide
If you kissed me now
my lips would taste just like cyanide
Press them against mine
See how we ruin things to pass time
Gasping for breath and caught under
A flagellating, ritual landslide

Feel So Real

Why don't we touch
Like humans in love?
Even if it is make-believe?

Why don't we kiss
Like humans that have missed each other?

The Pianist

Hiding her countenance behind thick,
  uncombed hair
Matted stage curtains
Fingers moving so fast, they blur in action
In the middle of the station
A symphony

Passers-by
either deaf to her melody
or inconvenienced by it

A station guard shuts the lid of the piano
Wood nipping at the tips of her fingers as they
retract hastily from the keys she has learned over a lifetime
to caress
and manipulate
Causing the inanimate body
to sound explicitly at her touch

Shooed away like a rodent
'Vermin Virtuoso'
She left the stool
and shed her confidence as if it were a jacket

Hold the Moment Like a Child

Young eyes
I want to see what you see
Young eyes
I want to dream how you dream

To hold the moment like a child
With the clumsy tenderness of a first-timer
Forgetting with amnestic forgiveness
A blank canvas causing clown-like happiness
Salted tears simply hushed or rocked away
Believing without question
Befriending without judgement
Creating without doubt
Sharing without inhibition
Fearing the vivid pretend
And not the serpentine solidity of reality
which slithers in the distance
The clothes-pile creature
More threatening than man, for now
Daddy is the safety word
in the foreverness of
our duvet kingdom

Young eyes
I want to see what you see
Young eyes
I want to dream how you dream

The Theatre of Contorted Reality

A standing ovation
in the theatre of contorted reality
Five-star reviews across the board
For the dexterity with which
You have so effortlessly distorted
and remoulded yesterday
Until it has become your truth
A plaything to twirl absent-mindedly between your fingers
We watch the baton dance
Before you pull the trigger
A slick assassination of character
Who befalls the unfortune of landing the lead role
in a plot as pliable as putty?
As inconsistent and unreliable as
Train wi-fi
British weather and
Memory?
Your truth
is
just another lie
Waiting to be uncovered

Ephemeral Eternity

Forever is a fiction.

I wish that I could preserve us time-capsule tight

Embalm our embraces

Suspend and stretch the seconds we spend together

In some sort of

cloying cryosleep

I could never get enough of you,

When eternity is ephemeral

Lightning Source UK Ltd.
Milton Keynes UK
UKHW052221200922
409177UK00001B/16
* 9 7 8 1 7 3 9 1 0 3 0 1 9 *